Original title:
Meaning in the Middle of the Madness

Copyright © 2025 Creative Arts Management OÜ
All rights reserved.

Author: Sebastian Whitmore
ISBN HARDBACK: 978-1-80566-005-7
ISBN PAPERBACK: 978-1-80566-300-3

Beneath the Surface of Strife

Beneath the chaos, cats lay sprawled,
Life's a circus, and we're enthralled.
Juggling socks and cups of tea,
In this wild act, we find glee.

Chickens dance with disco flair,
While squirrels plot in the old oak chair.
Straws keep twirling, drinks can spill,
Laughter echoes, what a thrill!

Bananas slip, but spirits thrive,
In wacky moments, we all jive.
A circus tent made of our dreams,
With balloon animals bursting at the seams.

So let the noise swirl all around,
In this playful whirl, joy is found.
Hold tight to humor, let it shine,
Beneath the strife, we're all just fine!

Navigating the Narrow Maze

Round the corners, what do we spy?
A hamster drifting, oh my, oh my!
The cheese is missing, plot thickens fast,
In this narrow maze, we're set to blast.

Zebras wear the silliest hats,
While raccoons dance with vibrant spats.
Lost in this fun, we laugh so hard,
In the merry mess, we're never scarred.

Mice with maps, but still they roam,
Finding adventure far from home.
With laughter echoing, spirits soar,
In this madness, we always want more.

Twists and turns, a giggle parade,
Navigating the quirks, unafraid.
So join the fun, let worries phase,
In our silly world, we'll never graze!

Taming the Tempest

In a whirlwind of socks and dreams,
I chase after time, or so it seems.
The kettle's on, it starts to dance,
While I ponder fate and casino chance.

With coffee spills and giggling cats,
I juggle chaos, and wear my hats.
Life's a circus, with pies that fly,
And I'm just a clown, giving it a try.

The Joy of Being Present

At breakfast, the toast did a flip,
I laughed so hard, I dropped my grip.
Fruit flew high, a juicy mess,
I welcomed chaos with a warm caress.

The alarm clock honked, a rude surprise,
Yet I find magic in tired eyes.
Each moment juggles its quirky charm,
Like a kitten sprawled, causing no harm.

Ballet of the Baffled

I pirouette in mismatched shoes,
Tripping over yesterday's news.
Dancing with the dust bunnies near,
A graceful twirl, then a sneeze of cheer.

With every misstep, the crowd just roars,
As I leap through laundry room doors.
Life's a dance, though I fall flat,
Who knew the floor could be so fat?

A Breath of Perspective

In the chaos of things left undone,
I pause to marvel at clouds in the sun.
A deep breath in, a giggle out,
Rediscovering joy in that little doubt.

In a world where nothing makes sense,
I balance my woes on a pickled fence.
Life's quirks are a grand buffet,
And I'll feast on laughter, come what may!

Resilience in the Ruckus

Amidst the chaos, I trip and fall,
But laughter's the splint that strengthens all.
With eggs on my face, I dance in the fray,
Life's messy, but hey, it's a wacky ballet.

Each twist and turn, like a clown on the run,
Spinning my troubles, we're here for the fun.
The world throws pies; I juggle and cheer,
In this carnival, panic has no place near.

Moments of Lucidity

In a whirlwind of socks, I find a shoe,
A moment of clarity, who knew it's blue?
With toast in one hand and coffee in stride,
I laugh at the mess, let the chaos collide.

The cat gives me side-eye, a true critic's gaze,
While searching for sense in this puzzling maze.
Yet in fleeting seconds, when silence is near,
I chuckle at life, with a wink and a cheer.

Searching for Stillness

In a storm of socks and a flurry of hats,
I seek out a corner, escape from the spats.
With a yawn and a stretch, I flop on the floor,
Serenity's hiding behind the back door.

But then there's a hiccup, a sneeze, and a giggle,
Turns peace into laughter; I skip, I wiggle.
The circus of life spins wildly around,
While I wear a grin, it's madness unbound.

Grace Under Pressure

When the world's upside down and the dog steals my snack,
I toss him a chip, it's just a small crack.
With chaos as my dance partner, we twirl and we spin,
Each misstep a jiggle, let the laughter begin.

With cake on my nose and my hair in a frizz,
I juggle my duties like a fun-loving whiz.
Though pressure may rise, and the clock runs so fast,
I pirouette through it all, and make moments last.

In the Heart of the Tempest

Winds howling loud, a laugh in the storm,
Crazy hats flying, a whimsical norm.
Umbrellas turn inside out with a cheer,
Dancing in puddles, we shed all our fear.

Lightning's the spotlight, thunder's applause,
We tango with raindrops, just because.
In chaos we find, a rhythm or two,
And leap through the madness, with nary a clue.

A Tapestry Woven with Disarray

Threads of bright colors, all jumbled in knots,
A cat in the yarn, tying up all our thoughts.
Laughter erupts as we trip on a stitch,
Crafting our chaos, a glorious glitch.

Each corner we turn, there's a bump in the road,
A bicycle's honking, a clever old toad.
With misfits and mishaps, our hearts tightly race,
In the mayhem of life, we still find our place.

Still Waters Beneath the Rush

Beneath all the splashes, a calm little spot,
Where ducks in top hats are breeding a plot.
A fish with a bowtie swims by wearing glee,
While chaos above keeps them all in a spree.

With whispers of ripples that giggle and glide,
We float on bright noodles, enjoying the ride.
The world may be spinning, but here we remain,
Sipping on lemonade, ignoring the rain.

The Unseen Symphony in Confusion

Bells ring and the banjos all strum out of tune,
A squirrel plays drums as it dances with a spoon.
The cacophony swirls, so wild, yet so grand,
In the mess of the music, we find a new band.

Feathers and feathers, a trumpet that squawks,
A lively parade of bewildering blocks.
Through giggles and grumbles, we join the charade,
In the chaos of sound, our joy is displayed.

In the Crooked Path, a Compass

A penguin wearing a top hat,
Waddles clumsily on the mat.
With a map upside down, oh dear!
He still thinks adventure is near.

Each twist and turn makes him laugh,
Until he tripped on a giraffe.
The compass spins with frantic zeal,
He shouts, 'At least I've got good feel!'

Shards of Hope in the Fray

In a circus tent made of cheese,
Clowns juggle dreams with such ease.
Pie in the face, oh what a sight,
Laughter erupts, all feels just right.

Confetti rains down from the skies,
As elephants twirl, oh what a prize!
Amidst the chaos and the play,
Shards of joy sweep fears away.

The Art of Balancing on the Edge

A juggler on a seesaw tight,
Wobbles left and wobbles right.
With feathered hats and shoes so bright,
He dances with a charming fright.

Balancing is truly an art,
Like fixing a sandwich on a cart.
Each slip a comedy so grand,
Who knew chaos could be so planned?

Where Turbulence Meets Tranquility

A wild unicorn named Sue,
Paints rainbows in shades of blue.
She tumbles and yelps with delight,
Chasing butterflies in flight.

In the chaos, she twirls around,
Finding joy on shaky ground.
With every bounce, the world spins fast,
In silliness, her hopes are cast.

The Thread of Connection

In a room full of chatter, I lost my shoe,
The cat on the table just laughed, who knew?
Spinning in circles, I can't find my hat,
While the fish in the bowl judges me flat.

Jokes fly like popcorn, the mood's in the air,
Balloons float by, and who even cares?
A tangle of limbs in a dance of delight,
We laugh at the chaos, it feels so right.

When Noise Becomes Music

Sirens serenade as I dance down the street,
With a tin can drum, oh what a beat!
Ducks quack along to the symphony strange,
Life's a cacophony, isn't it change?

When spoons become shakers, and laughter's the key,
I waltz through the ruckus, just feeling so free,
Each sound is a note in this playful parade,
In the din of it all, new friendships are made.

Silent Seams of Understanding

While mops do the tango and chairs seem to glide,
The hiccuping laughter we cannot hide,
A wink and a nod say more than the words,
Connecting in silence, like synchronised birds.

The chaos of chatter becomes a soft hum,
Pajamas at meetings? Oh, isn't that fun?
As we laugh at our blunders and trip over dreams,
In this wild, silly world, nothing's as it seems.

Finding Flow in Upheaval

Spinning plates teeter as I juggle my wits,
Unruly surprises give life little fits,
Tripping on laughter, I catch my own fall,
In the dance of the frantic, we're having a ball.

The blender's a DJ, spinning tunes of the day,
With sprinkles of chaos that just want to play,
When the world turns upside down, I've got my groove,
In the swirl of the mad, I find my own move.

Whispers Amidst the Storm

In a world where cats wear hats,
And dogs discuss philosophy.
The squirrels debate with acrobatic feats,
While the pigeons plot a grand spree.

With umbrellas upside down, they dance,
Chasing raindrops, slipping with glee.
A tornado of laughter spins in the air,
As we sip tea with a side of spree.

Jokers juggling thoughts on their toes,
While the frogs croak their own serenade.
The chaos swirls in delightful jest,
As the wacky wind joins the parade.

Yet in this slapstick whirlwind of cheer,
We find joy in the silly and sweet.
Amidst the wildness, a chuckle rings true,
And life becomes a whimsical treat.

Finding Light in Shadows

When shadows play hide and seek,
And the moon wears a grin so wide.
The bats wear ties at the last nightcall,
While owls share jokes with their pride.

In corners where giggles reside,
A brightness flickers like a spark.
The night turns into a carnival,
As we dance and sing till it's dark.

A funny little cat tiptoes by,
With a feather duster in her paws.
She sweeps away the seriousness,
While the fireflies applaud with their applause.

So here's to the laughter that must be found,
In shades where the oddballs convene.
For life gains color in the quirky,
And shadows shine with jolly sheen.

Navigating Through the Noise

Amidst the clatter and chatter loud,
The toaster's singing in the kitchen.
While the fridge hums a tune of delight,
And the blender's trying to switch in.

The television bickers with the clock,
While the dog rolls his eyes in a glance.
A parade of pots and pans join the fun,
As they all join in a joyous dance.

In this clamoring symphony we share,
A butterfly flits, oblivious to stress.
The chaos harmonizes quite well,
When laughter turns it into a jest.

So take a step back, embrace the sound,
Find the connection in playful banter.
For in this ruckus, hearts intertwine,
Creating joy from the wildest canter.

Harmony in the Hectic

In the rush, the madcap rush of life,
Where coffee spills on papers galore.
A dancer twirls with a fleeting shadow,
While the clock giggles, asking for more.

The cat jumps from table to chair,
Chasing dreams among stray balloons.
A symphony made of hurried hearts,
Plays along with our favorite tunes.

As laughter resonates off the walls,
We juggle chaos like a grand show.
With every awkward little mishap,
We craft a tale that will surely glow.

So in this hectic, hilarious spree,
Let's find the rhythm in all our folly.
For joy is a state of merry embrace,
And we'll never feel quite so jolly.

The Palette of Pandemonium

In a world that's upside down,
Colors swirl without a sound.
Splashes of chaos, a vibrant hue,
Painting smiles, laughter too.

Mixing joy with a dash of strife,
A canvas of quirky, crazy life.
Brushes flick, oh what a spree,
Dancing splatters wild and free.

Around the corners, giggles bounce,
Tickling toes, the heart will flounce.
In this mess, we find our grace,
A masterpiece in this mad race.

With every scribble, stories bloom,
Whimsical scenes in every room.
Laughing through the tangled thread,
Creating joy, enough said!

Crafting Calm from Chaos

In a whirlwind of squeaks and squeals,
Where the zany mix with clumsy heels.
Mastering chaos with a cup of tea,
While juggling penguins, 'Come dance with me!'

Potted plants in hats ask why,
As the cupcakes laugh and start to fly.
We sip our brews, all froth and foam,
In this ruckus, we find a home.

Sticky notes like butterflies,
Flapping wings as they criticize.
Yet, in the giggles, sense unfolds,
Wisdom hidden, brightly bold.

Through the clutter, we thread our way,
Finding calm amidst the play.
With every hiccup, giggling loud,
We craft a peace, a joy that's proud!

Out of the Fray

In the jangle of a noisy street,
Frogs in top hats try to eat.
While bouncy balls skip past the trees,
Laughter floats on the buzzing breeze.

Twirling leaves, a merry band,
Playing tag, hand in hand.
A juggling cat dons a bright bow tie,
As giggling puppies leap and fly.

Out of the fray comes a joyful laugh,
A whimsical twist on a silly path.
Turning chaos into a dance,
Every oops is a brand new chance.

So here we are, nothing's amiss,
In this rumble, there's pure bliss.
With every chuckle, we weave our tale,
In this funny adventure, we shall prevail!

Emerging from the Echoes

From the echoes of clattering shoes,
To the whispers of mischievous hues.
Where the pancake flips and the spaghetti twirls,
Amidst the giggles, the laughter unfurls.

Bouncing socks and a cat with flair,
Twirling about without a care.
Banana peels on the kitchen floor,
Each slip a dance, who could ask for more?

Emerging bright from a swirl of sound,
Finding joy in the unbound.
The silly faces and wiggly taunts,
In this circus, every heart flaunts.

So let's embrace the joyful mess,
In the chaos, we truly bless.
With laughter as our guiding thread,
We'll paint the world with smiles instead!

Awakening Within the Storm

In chaos' joyful whirl, we spin,
Chasing our tails, where to begin?
Umbrellas upside down, we laugh,
As puddles splash in our photograph.

Rain drops tap-dance on my head,
While cows float by, what was said?
Laughter breaks through thunder's roar,
In this wild ride, we'll ask for more.

A sunbeam tries to peek and grin,
But lightning's flash has joined the din.
Butterflies swim in swirling air,
In the storm, we find our flair.

So grab your boots, come join the ride,
With rubber ducks and giggles wide.
Each twist and turn, a gleeful tease,
Within this ruckus, we find our ease.

Serenity's Subtle Dance

Amid the chatter, chaos reigns,
Foot tapping, lost within the trains.
A napkin flies, it makes a dive,
Yet in the ruckus, we feel so alive.

Teacups spin in dizzy delight,
Jelly beans roll away from sight.
In the mischief, a waltz begins,
As smiles spread wide, the laughter wins.

The clock runs fast, it's running late,
But we just shrug, who cares? It's fate!
With every sip, we find the cheer,
In silly moments, peace is near.

So join the whirlwind, sway and sway,
In this dance, let worries stray.
With every twirl, the world expands,
Serenity blooms in vibrant bands.

Pieces of Truth in the Tumult

In the noise, there's a secret song,
Where fish ride bikes and donkeys prong.
Giraffes cartwheel beneath the sun,
In the wild ruckus, we find our fun.

A whirlwind of socks, oh what a sight,
As we juggle dreams with all our might.
With rubber chickens, we drop the truth,
In laughter's embrace, we find our youth.

Socks on our hands, we wave and boast,
While juggling dreams, we toast and toast.
Misfit thoughts in a pillow fight,
In this crazy mess, everything's bright.

So grab a silly hat, come on and play,
In the tumble of truth, we laugh away.
Life's pieces scattered, we just embrace,
Finding joy in the wildest space.

Voices Through the Bedlam

Hey there, friend, do you hear the beat?
That's chaos marching on silly feet.
Whispers of wisdom wrapped in glee,
Ask the prancing cat what's meant to be.

In the muddle, a parrot squawks,
"Dance with the mice, ignore the shocks!"
With each shout, a giggle breaks free,
In the din, we ignite a spree.

A rubber band snaps, oh what a sound,
As jokes on stilts dance all around.
In the wild mess, let laughter ring,
Through all the bedlam, joy takes wing.

So shout it out, join in the fun,
When life gets mad, we'll not be done.
For in this uproar, we find a way,
To laugh together, come what may.

Harmony in the Hectic

In the hustle, I dance with my shoe,
Tripping over bags, oh, what a view.
Coffee spills, but I laugh and twirl,
Lost my keys? Just another swirl.

Traffic jams are a wacky show,
Honking horns in a symphony flow.
Each fender bender, a giggle and grace,
Life's a circus, let's join the race.

Juggling schedules like a clown on parade,
Late to the meeting? I'm not dismayed.
Weave through the chaos, a humorous plight,
With laughter as armor, we'll win this fight.

In crowded spaces, I'll find my beat,
Join the chaos; it's a hilarious feat.
Even when wild, let joy ignite,
In the hectic, we'll find delight.

Serenity in the Shattered

Shattered dreams in a coffee cup,
I sip slowly, won't give up.
Broken mornings, but I still cheer,
Who knew chaos could feel so dear?

Pancakes flipped but always miss,
Syrup drips, oh what a bliss.
Mismatched socks, a fashion bold,
Life's quirks are treasures to hold.

In the wreckage, I find my laugh,
A lost direction leads to a path.
Cracked mirrors? I'll strike a pose,
Find the fun in every dose.

Dancing through spilled milk and cheer,
With every oops, I hold life near.
In chaos' arms, I twirl and zip,
Finding joy on this wild trip.

Threads of Calm in the Turmoil

Turmoil's here, but let's not pout,
Let's knit a scarf through this rout.
Yarn tangled but I'm not stressed,
Laughing at chaos, I feel blessed.

Spinning plates in a comical whirl,
Dancing sideways, give it a twirl.
Life's a puppet on strings so tight,
But guess what? We're ready to fight.

In tangled threads, we'll find our rhyme,
Witty verses in the silliest clime.
Laughing at mishaps, oh what a thrill,
In this chaos, I find my will.

Amid the ruckus, a smile so bright,
Embracing the mess feels just right.
With wit like glue, I hold tight to grace,
In the turmoil, I find a warm place.

The Eye of the Whirlwind

In the eye of the storm, I wear a hat,
Swirling winds can't handle that!
Twisting and turning in frolicsome flight,
Finding the bright in the darkest night.

With clouds that dance and thunder's roar,
I plunge into laughter, who could ask for more?
Rain's pouring down, but I'm still here,
Splashing in puddles, let's spread the cheer.

The whirlwind spins, I'm not feeling frail,
Riding the gusts, I'll never derail.
Giggling through chaos like a bold kite,
Even in madness, life's pure delight.

So take a bow in this blustery show,
With humor in hand, let laughter grow.
The wild winds can swirl and they will, you see,
In the heart of the storm, I'm happy and free.

Beneath the Rush

In a world where clocks tick loud,
I trip over laughter, lost in the crowd.
My coffee spills, a symphony bright,
Chasing the chaos with all of my might.

Birds wear hats, oh what a sight,
Chirping tales of pure delight.
Cats do the tango on the floor,
Life's a dance, who could ask for more?

Emails flood like pigeons in flight,
I reply with a wink, it feels just right.
The boss is juggling, and I can't stop,
Let's take a break! I'm ready to pop.

Beneath the rush, the jesters play,
Injecting joy in the mundane fray.
With every slip, a giggle escapes,
Finding calm in these funny shapes.

Sweeping Away the Static

Riding waves on a vacuum, how bold!
Dust bunnies dance, their tales unfold.
I saw a sock disappear with a grin,
The laundry has secrets, it's chaos within.

A cat in a hoodie, strutting with flair,
Claims he's the king of the living room chair.
While I ponder why my toast's upside down,
I chuckle at chaos in this little town.

Radio blaring the blues on a loop,
I sing off-key, join the merry troop.
A squirrel's audition for a starring role,
In the theater of madness, he steals the show.

Sweeping static with a feathery broom,
Comedic echoes fill every room.
Laughter bubbles like soda pop,
In this whirling tornado, we'll never stop.

Pause Amidst the Pulse

Juggling smoothies and work deadlines,
My blender's rumbling like wild train lines.
I take a sip, it spills down my chin,
And laughter erupts from within my skin.

The dog chases shadows, splendid delight,
While I fumble in socks that don't match right.
Finding joy in the slip and the slide,
In the madness, let the silliness ride.

Notifications ping like a wild parade,
I wave to the madness, join the charade.
Pineapple on pizza? Oh what a dare!
In this nutty world, let's share a laugh, share.

Pause amidst the pulse, let's have a ball,
Spinning in circles, we're having a ball.
As calendars whirl and chaos remains,
We find our giggles amid all the trains.

Beyond the Confusion

Chasing the cat who thinks he's a dog,
We tumble together in a constant fog.
Pancakes flying while the toaster sings,
Welcome to breakfast, where madness springs.

Neighbors practice their karaoke skills,
I join the chorus, no time for thrills.
Is it Tuesday? Oh dear, who can tell?
In this wacky rhythm, we revel and yell.

Umbrellas twirl in the dancing rain,
As ducks parade, we frolic like trains.
Lost in the shuffle of socks and shoes,
We find a treasure buried in the blues.

Beyond the confusion, there's pure delight,
Silly moments that take flight.
We'll laugh at the chaos as day turns to night,
In this nutty journey, everything's alright.

Ripples of Reflection

In a pond of silly thoughts,
Frogs wear hats, they dance and prance.
Turtles plot their midnight quests,
While fish sing songs of romance.

Ripples spread, the laughter grows,
As ducks debate the finest shoes.
With every splash, a giggle bounces,
In this world, we share our blues.

Each bubble pops with silly truths,
The moon giggles at the chaos.
In this madness, life unfurls,
Creating joy, an endless gloss.

So raise a glass to crazy dreams,
And toast to life's absurd ballet.
For in the ripples, we find joy,
In laughter's glow, let's dance and sway.

The Still Small Voice

Amidst the noise of everyday,
A whisper calls us, soft and sly.
It tickles ears with funny tales,
As we all rush, it winks goodbye.

In crowded rooms where laughter reigns,
A lilting chuckle drops like rain.
It reminds us not to take a spin,
In the whirlwind, joy's our gain.

Silly melodies float around,
Like lost balloons from silly clowns.
Dance like nobody's in the way,
For comedy in life astounds.

So listen close, let laughter rise,
In simple joy, our hearts surprise.
This still small voice brings light and cheer,
In craziness, our spirits fly.

Divining Clarity

A crystal ball with googly eyes,
Foretells the future in surprise.
It rolls its orbs in a comical way,
Unraveling truths with silly lies.

When chaos reigns and plans go awry,
A rubber chicken makes us cry.
Its quack brings laughter, brings a smile,
From chaos blooms our comedy pie.

In tangled lives where we all roam,
We find our way through humor's home.
With hiccups and mishaps, we embrace the ride,
And bravely leap beyond the foam.

For every bump is just a chance,
To tap your foot and join the dance.
In clarity's shine, we strip the fuss,
And in our hearts, we take a stance.

In the Heart of the Uproar

In the heart of bustling streets,
Where random socks could cause a stir.
Around the corner, mischief waits,
A cat in shades, a confident blur.

Amidst the shouts and honking horns,
A giggle breaks through all the scorn.
Like clowns in traffic, all aglow,
In madness, laughter is reborn.

With each silly act, the world collides,
Slipping on joy, the heart must glide.
As life throws curveballs, doused in fun,
We laugh together, side by side.

So here's to chaos, let's raise a cheer,
For in this uproar, we find what's dear.
With every joke, we stitch our days,
In this great circus, we're pioneers.

Twilight of Turmoil

In the throng of swirling shine,
Chaos dances, sipping wine.
Jesters laugh with painted grins,
While sanity's lost among whims.

Cats chase shadows on the wall,
While logic seems to take a fall.
The moon winks with a cheeky glow,
As we spin down this dizzy show.

Sprinklers sprinkle in the dark,
Tickling toes, igniting sparks.
Laughter erupts as fears take flight,
In this goofy, starry night.

So let the world swirl and twirl,
We'll laugh through every trouble and whirl.
With each hiccup, we find a way,
To dance on rooftops, come what may.

Echoes of Truth

In a room where wits are frayed,
Laughter echoes, unafraid.
Jokes collide like rubber balls,
Truth peeks out from crooked halls.

Whispers float on coffee steam,
Absurdity becomes the theme.
Dancing with our silly flaws,
Life's a circus lacking pause.

Echoes bounce off splattered walls,
Tickling minds like playful calls.
In the chaos, clarity beams,
As we tumble through our dreams.

With every quirk that comes to light,
We find the joy in midnight fights.
So here's to truth, however absurd,
In wild laughter, it's all heard.

Roots Among the Ruins

Among the rubble, flowers bloom,
A garden grows in all this gloom.
Roots twist funny, hold on tight,
Laughing through the endless night.

In every crack, a story's told,
Of wacky days and nights so bold.
We trip on dreams that dance around,
In chaos, life's unexpected found.

Socks mismatched, we strut our styles,
Turning frowns into silly smiles.
With every turn, we dig some more,
Finding gems on the chaos floor.

So let us revel in this plight,
For roots in ruins bloom so bright.
In our laughter, we are free,
Creating joy in absurdity.

Courage in the Chaos

In swirling winds and flying hats,
Courage tips and giggles splats.
Balloons escaping in the fray,
Chasing dreams that float away.

With stumbles turning into dance,
We twirl around our crazy chance.
Clowns juggle hopes and silly fears,
As laughter drowns our hidden tears.

The chaos swirls, a playful friend,
Each mishap lends a funny bend.
In every mess, we find a way,
To giggle loud and seize the day.

So here's to courage, dressed in fun,
In every crazy thing we run.
We'll stumble bold through thick and thin,
Finding joy, let the madness begin!

Threads of Solace

In the whirlwind, I find my socks,
The left and right, two silly blocks.
Tangled tales of laundry spree,
Life's absurdity dances with glee.

Through scattered cups and lost remote,
My laughter floats like a friendly boat.
Chasing crumbs of joy beneath the chair,
Every mishap becomes a fair.

A cat that plots my next big fall,
While dinner's burning, I heed the call.
With tipsy mugs and quirky spoons,
I'm living life beneath the moon.

So raise a toast to what's askew,
In chaos, I find my jolly crew.
With every twist, a playful thread,
In this circus, I'm happily led.

Amidst the Turbulence

Balloons take flight in a bustling crowd,
I've lost my hat, but I'm feeling proud.
With ice cream drips down my shirt,
I join the mayhem, feelings convert.

Juggling work along with my snack,
Life's a circus, but I won't turn back.
My to-do list flies high like a kite,
In every blunder, there's pure delight.

Tea stains bloom like abstract art,
In chaos, I play the leading part.
Running late with mismatched shoes,
Every moment, I gladly choose.

So here's to life's ridiculous spree,
With a laugh, I set my spirit free.
In the madness where humor stays,
I'm dancing amid the wild displays.

Silent Echoes of Purpose

Fumbling through my cluttered desk,
Where lost ideas become a quest.
Post-it notes like butterflies,
Whispering secrets in disguise.

With coffee spills and doodles grand,
I chart my thoughts with a clumsy hand.
A plan to conquer the week ahead,
Yet life just laughs, full of dread.

Echoes of laughter bounce off the walls,
In the echoes, sanity calls.
I search for sense in tangled dreams,
Finding joy in the silliest schemes.

So with a sigh, I embrace the jest,
In the chaos, I'm truly blessed.
Amidst the silence of this clown,
I find my purpose upside down.

Glimmers of Hope in the Fray

Poking fun in the morning rush,
With mismatched socks, I greet the blush.
My cereal's dancing, what a feat,
In chaos, there's music, oh so sweet.

A rubber chicken leads my way,
Through crowded streets, I boldly sway.
Emails piling like a bad review,
Yet my grin says, 'Oh, how do you do?'

Tripping over laughter and old regrets,
I gather smiles, no room for debts.
With every stumble, I rise anew,
Finding the sparkle in every hue.

So here's to joy in the messy strife,
With quirky moments, I savor life.
For in each giggle, trust the sway,
A tease of hope in the fray.

Chaos and Clarity

In the jumble, socks whirl away,
A dance of laundry choreographed by stray.
Cats in the air, have lost their grace,
While I sip coffee, in total disgrace.

Dishes tower like a monument high,
I swear they wink as I just walk by.
The dog plays fetch with an old shoe,
Who needs sanity? I'm thriving, it's true!

My plants have opinions; they're thriving too,
They gossip about the chaos I brew.
Running in circles, I trip on my feet,
Yet somehow, this madness feels so sweet.

Laughter erupts, what a lovely mess,
In mayhem I find, life's quirky finesse.

The Stillness Between Storms

Raindrops tap dance on my windowpane,
Birds dive for cover; I can't help but feign.
An umbrella's a puzzle that I can't figure,
So I stroll outside, drenched, feeling bigger.

Lightning flashes, then silence reigns,
I stand with wet socks, but wisdom remains.
The world swirls to its tempestuous tune,
And I find my joy, quite out of tune.

Puddles become mirrors; I leap with a grin,
Reflecting my chaos, the laughter within.
I hear thunder chuckle, a jester it seems,
And in the storm's heart, I stroll with my dreams.

Yet in the calm, there's a whimsical fact,
That here in the mess, there's not a subtract.

Finding Light in Darkness

The lights went out; now I cannot read,
My snack stash becomes a wondrous seed.
A flashlight's glow, my latest delight,
I'm the queen of the shadows, ready for flight.

Monsters may lurk in the depths of the room,
But they're just waiting for the snack's fragrant bloom.
I dance with the echoes, my heartbeat's a drum,
In this goofy ballet, I'm totally numb.

Ghosties are giggling; I'm laughing away,
What's life without jests in a game we don't play?
I shout to the darkness, "Just bring on the fun!"
In the twist of the night, I'm the boisterous one.

A sock puppet army joins in my quest,
Together we'll conquer, bring out our best.
With giggles and grins, we cast out the fright,
In this silly abyss, we still find the light.

Whispers Amidst the Howl

Winds howl like banshees, a wild choir's song,
Yet in that tempest, I've learned to be strong.
The trees are swaying with unbridled zeal,
And I join their dance, making chaos a deal.

My cat is a pirate, on a rumpled bed,
Chasing shadows of ghosts that dance in my head.
With every thunderclap comes a furious leap,
While I'm here chuckling, the chaos runs deep.

The neighbors peek out, all wide-eyed in fright,
But I raise a toast with my snack by the light.
"Here's to the whispers amid all the roar!"
This joyful pandemonium we surely adore!

So, let the storm rage, let the wild winds play,
I'll find joy in the madness, come what may.
In the giggles and shrieks, in the wind's crazy thrall,
I hear soft whispers, and I'm having a ball!

Embracing the Unraveled

When chaos reigns and socks go stray,
I wear my shirt inside out all day.
The cat's been plotting, I swear it's true,
While I just noodle, oh what to do!

A jigsaw puzzle with half the pieces,
Lost in the laughter, my heart releases.
Balancing spoons while I sip my tea,
In a world this wild, it's silly as can be.

My hair's a nest, I think it's a bird,
Chirping soft secrets that sound absurd.
Yet in this circus, I find the goal,
A wobbly dance to my happy soul.

With my mismatched shoes, I prance about,
Singing loud tunes that are silly, no doubt.
Embracing the chaos, like a grand parade,
In this twist of fate, my joy is made.

Echoes of Silence in the Clamor

In a coffee shop where cups collide,
I sip my latte with much pride.
The barista's juggling, oh what a feat,
While I'm dreaming of my next sweet treat.

Conversations clash like pots and pans,
I smile at strangers and wave my hands.
Amidst the chatter, a calm does bloom,
My noisy thoughts create a room.

A pigeon coos as it struts and poses,
It's a feathered diva with comical doses.
In the heart of the noise, I find my calm,
A chuckle here, a quirky charm.

So I'll raise my cup, and toast this mess,
To the delightful chaos that's anyone's guess.
With laughter ringing like a cheerful bell,
In this jumble, I've found my spell.

The Dance of Shadows and Sunlight

The sunlight flickers like a playful tease,
While shadows waltz in the whispering breeze.
I chase my laughter, it runs so free,
A comedic ballet of you and me.

Dancing around with quirky moves,
The garden gnomes watch, they've got grooves.
In a pirouette, I stumble slightly,
But who needs grace when you shine brightly?

A sunbeam tickles my silly hat,
My reflection grins, imagine that!
With every bounce, I find new heights,
In this dance of chaos, my spirit ignites.

The world spins wild, but I won't fret,
With shadows and sunlight, we've got a duet.
So let's twirl and tumble, in laughter entwined,
In this hilarious chaos, joy's easily mined.

Amidst the Roar, a Gentle Pulse

In the bustling streets where honks announce,
I dance to my rhythm, I leap and bounce.
The world is roaring, like a wild beast,\nYet in my heart
lies a giggly feast.

A dog in a tutu chases a cat,
While I sip my soda, just imagine that!
With every uproar, I celebrate more,
Finding the pulse under life's loud roar.

I mix up my orders, two desserts please,
And the waiter laughs, oh what a tease!
In cupcakes and sprinkles, I drop my strife,
Unearthing humor, it's the joy of life.

So let the chaos spin like a top,
In this loud masterpiece, I'll never stop.
With giggles and grins, around I shall twirl,
Amidst the clamor, it's my silly world.

Reflections in the Whirlwind

In a world that spins with glee,
A tiny bird sings, 'Look at me!'
Upside down and round it goes,
While the cat just stares and dozes.

Socks are missing, hats awry,
A dance-off with a butterfly.
Chasing shadows, laughing loud,
We embrace the chaos, so proud.

Bananas fly and pie does slip,
On this wacky, wild trip.
Spinning thoughts, a dizzy cheer,
What's the sense? Well, who's got time to fear!

Life's a jigsaw tossed around,
Pieces lost, but joy is found.
Embrace the fool in every day,
And find your fun along the way.

Sparks of Insight

In a mad dash to seize the day,
My coffee's gone—oh what a fray!
The toast jumps up, it's quite the sight,
A little thrill, then morning bite.

Chasing dreams with silly schemes,
Laughter bubbling like hot streams.
Who knew that chaos could ignite,
A brilliant spark, a silly light?

Puns and jests in every corner,
Each mishap makes a true performer.
Dancing wildly through the haze,
Finding joy in playful ways.

So toss your woes and grab a laugh,
Life's just one big goofy giraffe.
In this crazy, mixed-up game,
We'll dance, we'll sing, we'll celebrate the same!

The Calm Beneath the Clamor

Where sounds collide like sassy bees,
There's calm that hides beneath the tease.
A cat plays chess while dogs debate,
Who won the race? Oh, can't be late!

The radio's blaring, kids do shout,
But look, a goldfish starts to pout.
A moment's pause, a sideways glance,
We scribble joy in a silly dance.

Among the ruckus, a glimmer shines,
In tangled thoughts, a warmth entwines.
A giggle erupts, the storm calms down,
And all the noise wears a funny crown.

So let's embrace this wacky glee,
Amid the clamor, you'll find me.
With laughter bursting like a balloon,
We navigate the playful tune.

Unraveling the Unruly

The dog wore pants and jumped on chairs,
Cats took charge and made the flares.
With every mishap, we laugh and cry,
Balloons fly high, oh me, oh my!

Juggling dreams with pizza pies,
Laughter echoed through the skies.
One sock here, and one sock there,
In this circus, we've got flair!

Tangled memories, a playful knot,
In the chaos, wiser thoughts are caught.
Embrace the quirky, let it all show,
For through the scramble, our spirits grow.

So gather round, let's break the mold,
Life's a banquet of funny gold.
In the unruly, joy's the best,
Let's dance through life, forget the rest!

Beauty Born from Bedlam

Amidst the clatter, a dance breaks free,
Laughter spills out like a wild jubilee.
Chaos wraps round like a cozy shawl,
In the ruckus, we pirouette and sprawl.

Socks mismatched, we stride with flair,
Juggling dreams, without a care.
A symphony crafted from honks and shouts,
In the beautiful mess, true magic sprout.

Tea spills over, a splatter of cream,
Every blunder becomes quite the meme.
With every tumble, we find a new beat,
Dancing through life, no trace of defeat.

So let the world whirl, let the chaos reign,
In the topsy-turvy, there's love to gain.
From bedlam, we rise, with a wink and a grin,
In the joyous disorder, we always win.

Navigating the Noise

Lost in a world of clanging and clatter,
We laugh at the echoes, what's the matter?
With cups in hand, we wade right through,
Making the best of this wild zoo.

Whistles and honks, a raucous refrain,
We groove in the chaos, we won't complain.
With a skip and a hop, we dodge and weave,
In the orchestra of life, we believe.

Voices like raindrops, splattering around,
We gather the sound, make it profound.
Amidst the cacophony, we find our beat,
Synchronized madness, a rhythm so sweet.

So let the horns blare and the sirens yell,
We'll dance through the din, and cast a spell.
In the noise, we find a whimsical grace,
Navigating noise, we set the pace.

Fragments of Peace in Chaos

Quiet moments in the bustling fray,
Coffee cups clink, what a lovely display.
In cardboard boxes, hopes huddle tight,
Fragments of peace flicker like light.

Duck quacks mingling with the street's roar,
Each beaming smile opens a door.
Puzzle pieces from laughter stitched right,
Chaos dances under the moonlight.

Lost in the shuffle, we pull out a tune,
The wit of the world paints bright as the moon.
With each awkward jiggle, we melt our woes,
In the whirlwind of life, sweet surprises grows.

So here's to the silly, the odd, and the strange,
In the fabric of chaos, we'll never change.
Fragments of laughter, of peace, we shall seek,
Finding joy in the madness, unique and sleek.

The Quiet Resilience

In the ruckus, a chuckle blooms bright,
Resilience wrapped in pure delight.
With shades of humor, we navigate on,
Even when the day feels like a con.

Whirls of confusion, a circus or two,
Each wobble and tumble, a giggle breaks through.
Underneath the mayhem, we stand with cheer,
The joy of the curvy path draws us near.

In tangled missteps, we find our way,
With a sprinkle of spirit, we seize the day.
For laughter is armor, resilient and bold,
In life's ups and downs, our stories unfold.

So let's toast to the goofy, the wild, and free,
The quiet within the storm, a jubilee.
Through shouts and whispers, we thrive and grow,
In the spaces of madness, our light will glow.

Seeking Silence

In a world that spins with glee,
I search for calm, just me.
Laughter echoes, noise in flight,
Yet I crave a quiet night.

Pillows piled, I close my eyes,
Dream of hush beneath the skies.
A sock's rebellion, think it's sly,
But even socks can make me cry.

Dancing dishes spin beside,
They play the tune, I try to hide.
Humming fridges sing a song,
Yet all I want is peace all along.

So here I sit, my silent plea,
In this ruckus, let me be.
I'll hide away in laughter's show,
And find my peace in socks that glow.

The Core of Commotion

Amidst the whirlwind, chaos reigned,
With every laugh, my sanity waned.
Comets of joy fly 'round my head,
While my coffee tumbles, jokes unsaid.

In the corner, a cat does prance,
Chasing shadows as it dares to dance.
I watch the circus unfold with grace,
Feeling like a jester in this space.

Balloons are floating, a pie takes flight,
As rubber chickens jump with delight.
In the crazy, I might just see,
The spark of laughter sets me free.

So I twirl in this circus show,
Where silliness begins to flow.
Commotion's heart, so throbbing, yet light,
Who knew the madness could feel so right?

Finding Wisdom in Whirlwinds

Caught in a spin, my head's a mess,
But comedy blooms in the wild excess.
Wisdom winks from a jester's grin,
While my sock decides to join in.

Crumpets crackle, tea goes flying,
And in the chaos, I can't stop sighing.
A deep thought floats in a teacup swirl,
Like dandelion seeds that twirl and twirl.

Laughter's whispers echo 'round,
Like silly creatures unbound.
And while the world spins fast and bright,
I find my sense of wrongs that feel right.

So here's to wisdom wrapped in jest,
In this whirlwind, I feel so blessed.
I'll dance with folly and take a chance,
For in the madness, I find my prance.

Tranquil Thoughts

In the noise, I seek a thought,
A peaceful spot that can't be bought.
My mind's a party with a clatter,
But who knew chaos could be flatter?

Birds are squabbling at the feeder,
While I contemplate my next deed-er.
A squirrel debates how to climb,
And I ponder when to sip my lime.

While chaos reigns, I chuckle sweet,
As a dog performs a clumsy feat.
Eyes like saucers, ears on high,
In this ruckus, I want to fly.

Finding stillness, curled up tight,
In the frenzy, I hold on to light.
For laughter's echo just can't cease,
In each mad moment, I find my peace.

Breathing in the Bedlam

In chaos where the wild winds blow,
A jester spins, a comical show.
Pies fly past, laughter fills the air,
As we juggle dreams without a care.

Socks mismatched, a fashion faux pas,
Yet strutting proudly, laughing, hurrah!
The world's a circus, silly and bright,
In every blunder, we find delight.

To dance on tables, a blissful spree,
The fool's got wisdom, can't you see?
In lunacy's grip, we shimmer and sway,
Making merry in disorderly play.

A tuba taunts, a cat plays the keys,
Spin around twirling, we do as we please!
In bedlam's embrace, we find our glee,
As laughter and chaos become our decree.

Starlight in the Noise

In the buzz of a bustling street,
A marching band's offbeat, quite a feat.
Echoes of giggles in the clatter,
As we sip on soda, nothing else matters.

A hero made of jelly beans,
Dancing through life, bursting at seams.
The sky unaware, it twinkles above,
While we stumble round, guided by love.

We juggle thoughts like clumsy clowns,
Wearing each other's shoes with frowns.
Yet in this racket, a song is born,
A symphony strange, yet none forlorn.

Starlight laughs at our tangled fate,
In this mad caper, let's celebrate!
For joy hides beneath the noise so loud,
Dancing through life, we stand proud.

Waves of Wisdom in Distress

A rubber chicken sails the stormy sea,
While fish wear hats, just to be free.
The tides are swirling, a wacky affair,
With wisdom surfacing, as if from thin air.

In capsized dreams, we find open doors,
A rollercoaster, but who keeps the scores?
Each splash of laughter brews lessons anew,
In the whirlpool of chaos, we find what's true.

Whispers of sarcophaguses' delight,
These beckoning waves, not quite what they sight.
For every cringe, there's a wiggle and twist,
Unravel the cosmos, see what you've missed.

Ride the currents with a smile so wide,
For even in distress, we can take a ride.
Wait for that wave, let it sweep you away,
In the madness we cherish, come what may.

Dancing with the Disarray

Twisted tangles in the sunshine glare,
A muddle of shoes thrown in midair.
With wobbly legs, we shuffle and sway,
In the chuckles of clutter, let's dance away.

The clock strikes none, and time's gone askew,
But spin with the goofballs, what else can you do?
Spoons in our pockets, harmonicas rule,
At this kooky dance, we're all just a fool.

The floor's a mess, but it's fun, I swear,
With confetti cascading, a colorful fair.
As laughter erupts like popcorn's release,
We waltz through the storm, finding our peace.

Each blend of blunders, a twirling delight,
In the chaos of life, we ignite the night.
So laugh in the disarray, dance till you drop,
For in the absurd, we'll learn to flip-flop.

Finding Purpose in the Pandemonium

Amidst the chaos, we all chime,
Dancing through the chaos, one step at a time.
A cat in a hat, a dog with a shoe,
Who knew that life could be so askew?

We juggle our woes like bananas in flight,
Socks on our hands, oh what a sight!
Searching for reason in the silliest game,
We laugh a little louder, we all feel the same.

With pies in our faces, and cheer in our hearts,
Finding the joy where the madness imparts.
A sprinkle of laughter, a dash of delight,
Amidst the ruckus, we soar to new heights.

So here's to the mess, the mirth all around,
In this bumbling circus, our joy can be found.
With each little stumble, we grin and we spin,
In the pandemonium, that's where we begin.

Flickers of Joy in the Jumble

In a box full of puzzle pieces lost,
A jester appears, but at what cost?
He tickles our minds, makes us giggle and sway,
In the jumble of life, he brightens the day.

With shoes on the wrong feet, and hair like a clown,
He spins through the chaos, never wears a frown.
He finds little flickers in each tangled thread,
Where laughter erupts, and worries are shed.

With a wink of the eye and a pie to the face,
In this blend of confusion, we find our own space.
The joy is contagious, the laughter, a spark,
Flickers of happiness light up the dark.

So gather around, let your worries be few,
In this jumble of life, let the fun be your glue.
We'll laugh through the madness, and every misstep,
With joy in our hearts, we'll cheer up the next rep.

Blossoms in the Brawl

In the midst of the ruckus, where tempers may flare,
A flower pops up, but without any care.
It giggles and wiggles, beneath all the strife,
A bloom in the brawls, full of humor for life.

We wrestle with chaos, like socks in a fight,
Yet spring blooms remind us to smile with delight.
In the uproar of noise, we find moments sweet,
Where blossoms of laughter make life feel complete.

With a boisterous cheer, and a laugh shared in glee,
These petals of humor, they tickle the free.
As we tumble and tumble, and brawl with the zest,
We bloom in our chaos, we're truly the best.

So dance with the mayhem, twirl with the sound,
In the bows of confusion, let happiness abound.
In every wild brawl, let the blossoms unfold,
With laughter as armor, we're brave and bold.

The Gentle Ripple of Resolution

When waves of wild chaos crash at our door,
We ride on the tide, seeking peace evermore.
A gentle ripple begins with a grin,
With laughter as headwind, life's chaos can thin.

Like ducks in a pond, we waddle in line,
Spreading joy in the water, not much is a crime.
With each little splash, and each joyous cheer,
We find tranquil moments, each day of the year.

We may stumble and fumble, but look at us go,
In the dance of the mayhem, we catch the flow.
With giggles and chuckles, we steer through the storm,
In the gentle ripples, we find our true form.

So here's to the journey, embraced in the jest,
In the swirl of confusion, we give it our best.
With smiles as our beacon, brightly we shine,
Through the gentle ripples, all's perfectly fine.

A Star Amidst the Screams

In a world that spins and whirls,
There's a clown with brightly colored curls,
He juggles fears and wild delusions,
With laughs amidst all the confusions.

He dances while the chaos roars,
On the stage of life, he scores,
With each pratfall, he finds delight,
A star that shines through the fright.

With every scream, he takes a bow,
Ha! You thought I'd show you how?
Instead, I'll twirl and do a flip,
In this circus, let's take a trip!

So when life throws you its best joke,
Just laugh with me, don't be a bloke,
We'll find the spark in all the noise,
A star that dances, full of joys.

Alchemy of the Anxious Heart

In a cauldron, I toss my doubts,
With a dash of humor, the laugh erupts,
Boiling worries into fluffy clouds,
Anxiety? Just jokes in crowds.

I brew my potion, a splash of whim,
With giggles and snorts, I'll make it dim,
Each anxious twitch, a playful dance,
Who knew chaos could find romance?

While others fret, I spin in glee,
A jester's heart beats wild and free,
In every fumble, a gem we find,
Alchemy of the silly kind.

So raise a toast to the mixed-up thoughts,
In laughter's warmth, we've all been caught,
With every chuckle, we disarm the dark,
Turning burdens into a silly spark.

Lost in the Chaos

In the maze where giggles collide,
I lose myself in a joyful ride,
With rubber chickens and silly hats,
I strut around talking to cats.

Oh, what a whirl, I trip and tumble,
Through stacks of clothes, I laugh and fumble,
The microwave beeps like it's all ablaze,
But I'm busy crafting a circus craze!

Among the chaos, I spot a cheer,
A band of misfits, they draw me near,
Together we dance, we laugh, we scream,
Finding our way in a whimsical dream.

When life is wild and feels like a ride,
Just grab a buddy, don't run and hide,
We'll navigate through the loud and bizarre,
Finding joy in the chaos, our shining star.

Fragments of Clarity

Amidst the laughter, truths unfold,
With silly faces, we're bravely bold,
In fractured moments, we find our way,
Each chuckle clears the clouds of gray.

As popcorn pops and soda spills,
We gather wisdom from funny thrills,
A wise old sage in jester's guise,
With playful wisdom, opens our eyes.

In every stutter, a spark ignites,
Laughter leads us to delightful heights,
A puzzle pieced with giggles and cheer,
In fragments, we find what's truly dear.

So let us laugh at absurdity's dance,
In the bright chaos, let's take a chance,
For within each joke, a truth may dart,
Fragments of clarity in the jester's heart.

Seeker of Serenity

In the circus of life, we dance and cavort,
Juggling dreams like a clown in a sport.
Whispers of zen in a chaotic din,
A smile on my face, let the fun now begin.

Lost in a tumble, I trip on a shoe,
The laughter is loud, as I wave my 'adieu'.
Harmony crafted in the wildest of mess,
In this crazy ballet, I find my success.

Spinning in circles, my thoughts take a flight,
The sun has a giggle, the moon joins the bite.
With each little blunder, I cherish the ride,
In the whirl and the twirl, I let joy be my guide.

So here's to the seekers, the jesters, the wise,
Finding delight in the world's funny guise.
For in every mishap, there's laughter to greet,
And joy's a companion that's never discrete.

Embers of Understanding

Amidst the confusion, the sparks start to glint,
Fires of wisdom from jokes that we mint.
A tickle of thought, like a bee with a buzz,
In the haze of our chaos, we find what it was.

Chasing the shadows that flicker and play,
The punchline that salvages monotony's sway.
With a wink and a nod, we confuse and collide,
In the heart of the riddle where giggles reside.

As the mash of voices ignites in the air,
I stumble on laughter and flirt with despair.
Yet here in the clamor, I see life's sweet truth,
In the flickers of humor, we find joy in our youth.

So let's stoke the embers, let whimsy ignite,
In the chaos we foster, we'll shine oh so bright.
With a chuckle and cheer, let our spirits embrace,
For laughter, my friend, is what fuels the chase.

Chaos Organized

Like socks in a drawer, all askew and in fight,
I wrangle my thoughts in the dead of the night.
A giraffe in a tie takes a trip on a train,
And chaos, it giggles, while sanity feigns.

In the tangle of plans, a parade starts to bloom,
A chicken in query supplies comic relief in the room.
With crayons and glitter, my heart is a riot,
In this disorganized art, I see my own diet.

Scores of odd moments, like a puppet on strings,
We're flailing and flopping, yet joy always clings.
So raise up your glass to the glorious spree,
In the madness, I promise, we find victory.

So gather the giggles, mix laughter with glee,
For in this big jungle, we're wild and we're free.
Chaos we cherish, with humor as guide,
Together we stumble, forever side by side.

Between the Cracks of Turmoil

In the rubble of chaos, a stray cat will spring,
With a meow that's a hymn, and a dance fit for kings.
Collecting the giggles like pebbles and seas,
Between all the cracks, I find pockets of bliss.

The jester's performance brews laughter so grand,
As the world spins around like a comical band.
Clowns in the corners, with pies as their shield,
In moments of madness, our hearts are revealed.

I trip on my shoelace, do a little spin,
In a tangle of limbs, we're all wrapped up in.
With chaos for canvas, we paint and we play,
Between all the turmoil, we banter away.

So come join the revels, let's frolic and thrive,
In the weirdest of places, we're happily alive.
For laughter is sunshine that brightens the fray,
And in midst of mayhem, we dance night and day.

Light Through the Fractures

In a world where cats can fly,
And fish wear tiny hats,
We dance with socks upon our heads,
As laughter intersects with spats.

Juggling jellybeans with flair,
While sipping on some tea,
A banjo made of spaghetti,
Sings tunes of jubilee.

When life throws pies into the fray,
And chaos reigns supreme,
We twirl amidst that flying goo,
Chasing every silly dream.

Through all the craziness around,
A giggle holds the key,
For in the laughter, joy is found,
As happy as can be.

Finding Center in the Maelstrom

When tornadoes hug the rooftops tight,
And squirrels wear polka dots,
We waltz with spoons upon the floor,
Defying all the odds.

In the middle of a donut fight,
With sprinkles flying high,
We wear our frosting crowns with pride,
As flying cake slices sigh.

Wobbling on a pogo stick,
In a world that's gone insane,
We find our joy in marshmallow clouds,
And sing a silly refrain.

So grab your friends, it's time to play,
In the whirlwinds, we will shine,
Finding humor in the wild,
Life's punchlines are divine!

The Beauty of Disarray

Tea leaves danced upon the floor,
As loons in tuxedos sing,
The flowers sprout from pancake stacks,
And joy's a rather quirky thing.

Upside-down umbrellas fly,
In a windstorm full of cheer,
With rubber chickens clucking loud,
Their wisdom sweet and clear.

The art of chaos finds its thread,
In every silly sound,
With flapping legs and wiggling toes,
The happy hearts abound.

Through topsy-turvy, we will glide,
In the beauty of this show,
For laughter is the thread we weave,
In the madness, we can grow.

Calmness in the Commotion

In a room where giants jump,
And teacups dance on screens,
We twirl with socks upon our hands,
And live inside our dreams.

A pickle dressed as royalty,
Takes center stage for all to see,
While dancing with a rubber duck,
In perfect harmony.

The chaos can be quite a treat,
As cakes are thrown around,
In a whirlwind of delightful mess,
We find our solid ground.

So raise your glass of fizzy glee,
To moments weird and bright,
For in this joyful ruckus,
We find the stars at night.

Lost Notes of a Beautiful Melody

In a world of notes all scattered,
A cat plays piano, quite flattered.
The dogs join in, howling a tune,
While a frog croaks under the moon.

Each strum brings laughter, each fall, a cheer,
The milk spills over, but we've no fear.
A fiddle found, with a bow that's gone,
We dance like fools till the break of dawn.

A tuba rolls by, right out of a kit,
A sandwich plays drums; oh, what a hit!
The grand finale ends with a twist,
With socks on our heads, who could resist?

So here's to chaos, the joy that it brings,
With each funny note, our heartstrings it sings.
In the mess of sound, we find our grace,
In wild harmony, we take our place.

Journaling Through the Jumble

A pen rolls away, just like my thoughts,
Between coffee cups and tangled knots.
My diary opens to a blank page,
With doodles and dreams all fueled by age.

Spilled ink as a river, it flows and it leaks,
A starfish in slippers, oh, the best of weeks!
I scribble my musings on napkins and bread,
While a squirrel in glasses gives advice instead.

The world I see, quite mixed and absurd,
As my cat narrates every crazy word.
With stickers and stamps, each laugh's a delight,
Horizons painted in colors so bright.

At the end of the day, I chuckle and sigh,
In these moments of chaos, my dreams always fly.
Through jumbled pages, I find a clear path,
In the messiness, oh, there's always a laugh!

Whirlwind of Discovery

A tornado of socks, a blur in the hall,
Chasing a dust bunny, oh what a ball!
The cat tries to catch it, dives under the chair,
While I trip on my shoelace, who put that there?

In the whirlwind of life, we spin and we twirl,
With a cupcake in hand and a chocolate swirl.
The toaster pops up with confetti-like toast,
While I laugh at the week that I thought I'd lost.

A map made of crumbs leads to nowhere near,
Yet I find a treasure in that little smear.
With each wild adventure, I stumble and grin,
In the chaos, my laughter pulls me right in.

So let's spin through the madness, a dance oh so grand,
With joy as our rhythm and snacks on hand.
In every tornado, a giggle is found,
In this whirlwind of life, we're happily bound!

The Art of Quietude

In a room full of whispers, my hair's in a bun,
As a quokka recites, it's all in good fun.
A turtle plays chess with a snail for a mate,
So quiet, the echo's just teasing our fate.

In calmness, I find that the chaos does fade,
With a cupcake so still, and a delicate braid.
The fish spin their tales in the deepest abyss,
While the dog tells me secrets, a slobbery kiss.

A breath and a giggle amidst all the schemes,
Paints laughter in silence, like colorful dreams.
In tranquility's arms, I find every jest,
Like a rubber duck diving with pure-hearted zest.

Here's to the silence, the laughter it brings,
In stillness, we dance; it's not what it seems.
For in quietude's grasp, the chaos is sweet,
In the art of calm laughter, our joy is complete.

www.ingramcontent.com/pod-product-compliance
Lightning Source LLC
Chambersburg PA
CBHW051650160426
43209CB00004B/862